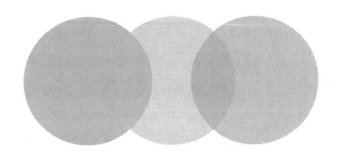

Fiona Brownlee and Lindsay Norris

Promoting Attachment
with a **Wiggle, Giggle, Hug** and **Tickle**

A Programme for Babies, Young Children and Carers

Jessica Kingsley *Publishers*
London and Philadelphia

First published in 2015
by Jessica Kingsley Publishers
73 Collier Street
London N1 9BE, UK
and
400 Market Street, Suite 400
Philadelphia, PA 19106, USA

www.jkp.com

Library of Congress Cataloging in Publication Data
Brownlee, Fiona.
  Promoting attachments with a wiggle, giggle, hug and tickle:
helping babies or young children and their
parents or carers / Fiona Brownlee and Lindsay Norris.
    pages cm
  Includes bibliographical references.
  ISBN 978-1-84905-656-4 (alk. paper)
1. Infants--Development. 2. Child development. 3. Attachment
behavior. I. Norris, Lindsay. II. Title.
  HQ774.B795 2015
  155.42'2241--dc23
                    2015000949

British Library Cataloguing in Publication Data
A CIP catalogue record for this book is available from the British Library

ISBN 978 1 84905 656 4
eISBN 978 0 78450 149 5

Printed and bound in the United States

Contents

●●●●●●●●● ● Acknowledgements

We would like to thank the following people for their continued enthusiasm and practical support in running the *Wiggle Giggle Hug and Tickle* programme:

Early years practitioners and managers of the Early Years Centres in Edinburgh, City of Edinburgh Council

Moffat Early Years Centre

Abbi Rouse for her illustration

Angela McLeman for her videography

Gael Munro, MEd. Chartered Teacher, who proofread the text and offered constructive amendments from an educational perspective

Eric Wood, BA, PGCE (FE), for his musical arrangements, vocals and photography

Our baby models (all of whom are under the age of two) Ava Strachan, Carys Brownlee, Heidi Norris, Leo Eggleston and Jay Macleod.

Our adult models David Norris, Carolyn Chiswick, Matt Strachan and Antonia Brownlee.

Lastly, we would like to offer a special thanks to all the parents, carers and children who have participated in our *Wiggle Giggle Hug and Tickle* programme.

Introduction

Background

This book was devised some years after the publication of our first book, which was dedicated to helping young children aged 2–5 with developmental and sensory processing difficulties as we became increasingly aware that there are few resources to help parents and carers[1] of children in the 2 months to 2 years age range.

In working as paediatric occupational therapists for many years, we recognised that some carers, particularly adoptive parents, long-term foster carers, and mothers suffering from post-natal depression and other mental health issues, can have difficulty identifying the needs of a baby in the early stages when getting to know them and forming a relationship.

The carer can struggle to understand what the baby is trying to communicate. Being able to tune in to, and read the signs from, a baby is not always instinctive or automatic. This develops when a secure attachment between the carer and baby has been established (we explain attachment in more detail in Chapter 1). When a carer engages and interacts with a child in a consistent, positive and fun manner, this helps the carer to learn what the child is trying to say. When the carer can read this from the child, and respond in a loving and consistent manner, the baby learns to trust the carer and a secure bond can develop.

Research shows that babies are born into the world ready to communicate, attach and show emotions.

Babies come into the world already connected to other people. This means that the capacity to be an engaged, relational being doesn't happen some time later in development, such as when children walk or talk or start school. This capacity is present from birth. Babies share emotional experiences. This means that how we, as adults, relate to our babies matters.[2] (Zeedyk 2012)

They come equipped with innate communication abilities and can imitate an adult when only a few hours old.

These opportunities should not be missed, and carers need to learn to read the signs a baby displays and respond accordingly. Babies understand long before they can talk.

. . . .

1   We have generally used the word 'carer' or 'caregiver' rather than 'parent' or 'mother' as the main caregiver may be the biological parent, grandparent, foster carer or adoptive parent. The term 'parental' includes parents and carers.

2   Zeedyk, S. (2012) Innate Connection. Available at suzannezeedyk.com/#/resources/ 4579047977, accessed on 19 May 2015.

The use of signs can help to develop a baby's comprehension and language and ability to communicate needs and wants without the use of words. Using signs to help the carer understand what her baby wants makes both carer and baby happy!

Research indicates that the more we invest in babies and pre-school children the better the rewards.[3] Brain scans show that babies who have suffered severe sensory deprivation have a much smaller brain than babies of the same age who have been appropriately stimulated, both emotionally and physically.

In the most extreme cases, this lack of stimulation can lead to dysfunction in cognitive, social and emotional areas in development. The 'return on investment' in pre-school children is significantly higher than in children of school age – the early years are the time to act. If we miss out at the start, the cost to society is enormous.

The first three years of any child's life matter dramatically and the first six months are most important of all. Babies' brains are born immature and need to be stimulated to grow. It is up to us as adults to programme this growth, as if we do not, the brain will wither and fail to grow as it should. It is an amazing fact that the synapses in the brain increase twenty-fold in the first three years of life!

There is a 75-year history of research into attachment theory and it continues to be important – the Chief Medical Officer for Scotland recently stated that we need to be even more aware of problems developing in children who miss out on early years attachments.[4]

The way in which our carers love us affects our ability to keep ourselves emotionally stable when we grow to become adults. Babies need consistent parenting in order to manage themselves in stressful situations later in life. This passes down from one generation to the next and any negative patterns must be broken.

A successful approach to improving this situation is by providing accessible and easy-to-follow community programmes and one-to-one support for carers. This book aims to meet this important need.

Everyone benefits: the baby, the carer and the professionals involved, as relationships develop with trust, confidence and understanding. As members

. . . .

3   Heckman, J. J. (2000) Invest in the very young. *Encyclopedia on Early Childhood Development.* Available at www.child-encyclopedia.com/Pages/PDF/HeckmanANG xp.pdf, accessed on 8 May 2015.

4   Sir Harry Burns, Chief Medical Officer in Scotland, headed up an early years collaboration. His analysis was printed in *The Times* newspaper on 12 January 2013.

of a community, we also require the support of the rest of our community to help us cope with the stress of raising children.

Governments are recognising the importance of training staff in attachment theory, thereby investing in future generations. Empathic parenting and play lay the foundations for a child to develop confidence and prepare them for school, which improves the wellbeing of society as a whole.

A recent project run in Scotland supports the proposal for more parental involvement in the early years to improve the health and wellbeing of both child and carer. Those carers benefiting from involvement in the programme were less stressed and had a better relationship with their child. Solid foundations for future generations cannot be understated.

We wish to promote parental and carer awareness of children's needs, to support parents and carers in their relationships with their children and to develop self-esteem, resilience and overall improvement in children's development. We want our children to grow up as confident, happy and secure adults who are able to cope with life's challenges. The *Wiggle Giggle Hug and Tickle* programme aims to address these issues in a fun way.

There is strong evidence to show that a lack of healthy interaction between carers and babies in the first year of life can be particularly problematic and cause long-term damage to a child's future physical and mental health.[5] The number of children suffering from Reactive Attachment Disorder (RAD) is larger than first thought, and this is often diagnosed much later on in life. RAD arises from a failure to form normal attachments to the primary caregiver in early childhood. This failure can result from severe early experiences of abuse, neglect and lack of responsiveness to a child's communication efforts. These children have had a very poor start in life for various reasons and their needs have remained unfulfilled. Such children can display various types of behaviour, either overly friendly towards, or extremely distrustful of, the adults whom they encounter in life. A harrowing statistic is that one in five children lives in a family where the carer has a diagnosis of some form of mental health problem. These children are even more at risk of suffering harm and neglect.

All carers need support and help in the early years of their baby's life, but some require more support than others. Building a strong attachment and bond between baby and carer is crucial. This also makes economic sense, and programmes for early intervention need to be universally available.

5   Howe, D. (2011) *Attachment Across the Lifecourse. A Brief Introduction.* Basingstoke: Palgrave Macmillan.

Participation in group programmes could either be recommended by health visitors or initiated by carers themselves who recognise that they would benefit from increased support and encouragement from early years practitioners.

The *Wiggle Giggle Hug and Tickle* programme has been run successfully in a group format for several years in Edinburgh. The programme has been planned and implemented to take account of the research findings in the area of attachment and early childhood development, and the feedback from those attending the classes has been extremely positive. The group has been run with biological parents, adoptive parents, foster carers, and grandparents. Group size can vary from two children up to ten; however, we believe that a maximum of eight children attending is enough as it is more challenging to run the group smoothly. Running the groups was fun and easy to do provided that you were prepared beforehand. The only outcome measures we have are anonymous completed evaluation forms from parents and other professionals who took part in a group.

Outcomes

The programme is designed to pay special attention to improving the bond between baby and carer; however, attendance on the programme offers many other benefits, not only for the child but also for the carer.

Children attending the programme are encouraged to develop their interest in games and participate in the activities. They also begin to learn basic social skills such as how to share, play with others, wait patiently, take turns and follow instructions. Interaction skills are developed by encouraging eye contact and supporting the child to make choices and develop anticipation skills. The programme also provides a way to help babies and young children to learn about transitions – when one activity ends and another one begins.

The programme is designed to have a clear beginning, middle and end so that it has a clear structure and children are able to familiarise themselves with it. Within the programme, children have an opportunity to engage in physical and sensory experiences as well as the use of signs and gestures as a form of communication. This is also an allocated time for the carer to simply be with her baby, providing the one-to-one attention that is so vital for strengthening the bond between carer and baby.

Carers learn how to 'read' their child. They can gain a greater understanding of what their baby is trying to tell them. They can become more attuned to their baby and pick up on the tiniest pieces of information that their baby is telling them – information that they may have missed previously. Carers should learn how to look for the non-verbal as well as verbal communication from their baby. They will also become familiar with various nursery rhymes, movement activities and sensory activities that they can continue to use at home. Carers may also share their own experiences and make friendships with other carers in the programme.

Both children and carers can, through having time set aside to play, communicate and simply have fun, and develop a positive relationship and a close bond.

Positive feedback

Whenever we run the programme, we ask the carers to complete an anonymous evaluation form. The feedback, whether good or bad, helps us to change and develop the programme for the better. These are some of the comments that we have received from parents and carers:

'I think that the programme is a good link to have the one-to-one with your baby because of our busy lifestyles and you also get to meet with other mums. I thoroughly enjoyed the sessions and I hope that there is another one soon. Thank you very much from me and my baby.'

'Great programme – I never knew that playing with my baby could be so much fun!'

'This programme really helped me to pick up on the subtle cues my baby was telling me, like when they had had enough of something or that they wanted more of it. There was so much that I was missing before because I didn't know what I was to look out for.'

'I have the children's television channels on for my wee one but I had forgotten just how important it is simply to sit with my child and sing to her myself. Thanks for reminding me.'

Below is a testimony from an early years practitioner:

'Moffat Early Years Campus has completed the *Wiggle Giggle Hug and Tickle* programme with a group of mothers and babies. The staff found the structure of the group easy to follow and the resources required are used on the Campus every day, therefore there was no requirement to buy anything.

The babies responded really well to the group and it was lovely to see them interacting with their carers and anticipating what was going to happen next. The babies enjoyed all the activities and it was quite astounding to see them respond so well to the use of sign language. This became apparent from the change in one baby's body language when staff asked her to "wait" using both the sign and word – the baby became still and focused on the member of staff until she heard "again?" then she became very animated and excited. The group encourages the babies to begin making choices from two things; seeing a five-month-old baby reach out to make a choice and seeing her face when she picked up what she wanted was very precious.

The feedback from the carers was very positive. They enjoyed the quality time with their baby and the opportunity to try new toys as they had not thought to try some of the items or how much fun they could have with just a balloon, all ideas of things they can do at home. I would thoroughly recommend practitioners who work in an early childcare setting to carry out the *Wiggle Giggle Hug and Tickle* programme as it was a joy to deliver.'

1

Attachment

Positive attachment

A positive attachment is when a caregiver develops an affectionate bond with her[6] baby by responding to her baby's needs and wants appropriately and consistently. It is important that a baby develops a relationship with at least one caregiver to enable his social and emotional development to occur normally.

The baby's mother is usually the main caregiver; however, this role can be undertaken by anyone who consistently behaves in a 'mothering' way. Babies can form attachments to any caregiver who is consistent, sensitive and responsive in her social interactions with them. This is how trust and relationships are formed. Other attachment figures, including the father, are also important for the child's wellbeing.

Mothers usually bond with their babies instinctively to help protect and care for them. Early bonding experiences give a child memories, beliefs, morals, expectations, emotions and behaviours. Children who experience positive attachment will have higher self-esteem by the age of three than children who experience negative attachment. The effects of attachment, whether good or bad, will last a lifetime. Children who have positive attachments with their caregivers, emotionally and physically, will most likely experience a similar bond with their own children. The positively attached child can begin to explore the world with the confidence that he will be supported and protected from serious harm and will be loved and comforted unconditionally.

Attachment is a process that takes time. Developing a secure attachment to the primary caregiver is extremely important as it is the foundation of trust that is carried on into adulthood.

Hormones and brain development

Social interactions have a massive part to play in a child's brain development. The most important parts of the brain to grow in the first year of life are those that are involved with the emotional and social functioning of the child. The way in which a child learns how to relate to other people, anticipate their actions and understand their feelings is the foundation of emotional development. In order for these parts of the brain to grow, emotionally enriched experiences are vital. Positive experiences help to embed positive brain development.[7]

. . . .

6   We have referred to babies and children as 'he' and to parents/carers as 'she' as generic terms whilst acknowledging that babies/children/parents/carers may be male or female.

7   Gordon, I., Zagoory-Sharon, O., Leckman, J. F., Feldman, R. (2010) 'Oxytocin and the Development of Parenting in Humans.' *Biological Psychiatry*, 68, 4, 377–382.

Brain cells are connected to one another in the brain. The brain cells process and transmit electrical signals when a cell is stimulated. When a signal is sent to a cell, it helps to embed that cell within the brain, making it readily available for use another time. For example, if a baby smiles then the baby gets a huge response from his mother. The baby thus learns that this action produces this positive response and the connections in the brain that are necessary to carry out this action again become stronger. However, connections that are rarely or never used will weaken, then shut down and will not function. This process is how the brain organises itself and grows, which happens most rapidly in the first two years of a child's life.

The dominant brain hemisphere is the right hemisphere. This is responsible for our social and emotional functions and empathy at an unconscious level. The interactive experiences that a child has with his carer will, undoubtedly, help to develop this area of his brain. Experiencing happiness is the key to attachment in the first year of a baby's life. A carer who shares in a baby's excitement and joy in exploration will stimulate brain growth.

A secure attachment between carer and child can generate release of high levels of the 'love hormone' oxytocin which, in turn, allows cells in the brain to grow. Oxytocin is a hormone that is released in mothers when they are in close contact with their baby in order to help mother and baby bond. The chemical release of oxytocin enhances maternal instinct. It helps to instil a highly responsive sense of protection, care and unconditional love in the mother so that she will nurture her baby to the best of her ability. The mother will be able to pick up on the non-verbal cues that her baby displays and will be more sensitive to his needs. Oxytocin also helps the mother to respond to her baby quickly and in a loving, calm manner. If she can do this, it will reduce levels of the stress hormone, cortisol, being released in her baby.

Reading your child

Babies are born with a powerful instinct that motivates them to stimulate as much care and attention as possible from their caregivers. The very first action from a baby is to cry. It is important that babies cry because this is how they influence others to look after them.

Carers have to 'read' their babies in order to know what they want or do not want. This means that the adult can read the non-verbal cues a baby will portray in order to let someone know how he is feeling. For example, if the carer tickles her baby and her baby laughs, the carer will know that her baby likes being tickled and she may tickle him again. However, should her baby turn away or close his eyes after the third or fourth tickling attempt, it may mean that he has had enough and the carer would know to stop. This is what we call 'reading your child'. If adult responses are provided to a baby in an appropriate and consistent fashion, and interactions are lively and fun, this helps to develop the bond between carer and baby. The quality of the interaction is more influential than the amount of time spent interacting. Another common interaction is smiling. A child begins to smile at an adult when he starts to link this facial expression with the delighted response he gets every time he does it. Babies as young as a few hours old can try to copy and model the facial expressions of their caregiver, but to continue this 'conversation' the carer has to be tuned in to what her baby is saying.

Empathy

If a carer can respond to her baby's cries for attention sensitively, swiftly, and in a predictable manner, her baby will begin to develop a confident and trusting relationship with her. If the carer is in tune in this way, and is able to read her baby's signals, the baby will develop a sense of secure attachment and high self-esteem. Her baby will then understand how another person feels towards him, which is essential for long-lasting friendships. Activities such as 'peek-a-boo' help to develop the vital sense of empathy between carer and baby. Empathy is the ability to connect with another person and understand their feelings and actions. When someone says, 'How would you feel if it were you?' or 'Put yourself in their shoes', they are asking you to empathise.

If a child has not had the opportunity to develop his basic sense of connection with others, he is much less likely to have empathy and, in turn, is not as likely to be protected against feelings of aggression. Children's disruptive behaviour, for example at school, can be due to alienation with regard to other people and can generate feelings of anger and resentment in response to not having their own needs met.

Negative attachment

There are different types of negative attachment, such as insecure avoidant, ambivalent and disorganised. These are all subgroups of Reactive Attachment Disorder. This can occur when a baby has been abused and ignored during his formative years. It is a result of trauma to the attachment process and is prevalent in babies who are adopted.

If a caregiver does not provide sufficient responsive and sensitive care to her baby, he may establish a negative attachment. A baby will eventually work out an attention strategy to attract optimum emotional care by modifying his nurture-seeking behaviour to the ability of the carer to respond. However, when the attachment figure is unresponsive (for example, due to depression or drug misuse), or if the attachment figure becomes violent and abusive, the child is left with no predictable strategy for enlisting enough comfort to form a predictable relationship.

If a baby feels that what he is trying to tell his caregiver is not being recognised, he may give up or try to achieve this in other ways. Negative social experiences then start to form a network of connections between brain cells. If these connections are reinforced on a regular basis, they will form stable structures in the brain, which can cause long-term, lifelong negative attachments. The child's mother or main caregiver should be the baby's security figure. The caregiver also needs to know how to calm, soothe and protect her baby. If the baby does not bond and have a secure attachment to the caregiver, then he will begin to behave differently in order to gain the appropriate attention of the caregiver (for example, if cries are not being answered, the baby may persistently cry).

The baby will try to protect himself from his caregiver. For example, if crying makes the caregiver upset or angry or the baby may rarely cry in order to avoid physical pain. It is only when a baby can develop a predictable and confident relationship with his caregiver that he will securely bond and connect with that caregiver. The first six months are crucial for developing attachment, but the signals must be reinforced for many months into babyhood.

Lasting effects of a negative attachment

The way in which children learn to interact with another person as a baby will influence their ability to make new relationships as they grow. Children who are negatively attached may have low self-esteem and may not feel worthy of the parental attention they crave. Such children also have an increased risk of becoming depressed, violent and prone to substance misuse.[8] As adults, they may have difficulty creating and maintaining relationships with friends or partners and they may also struggle to respond to the care of others, for example when someone is sick or grieving. Experiences of abuse and neglect, as compared with predictability and security, can have long-term negative consequences.

8   Leary, M. R., Schreindorfer, L. S. and Haupt A. L. (1995) 'The role of low self-esteem in emotional and behavioral problems: why is low self-esteem dysfunctional?' *Journal of Social and Clinical Psychology*, 14, 3, 297–314.

Resilience and emotional stability

Children need to feel secure and confident that their physical and emotional needs will be met in order to become resilient and independent adults who have the strength to overcome adversity. Some children can thrive even though they have experienced difficulties in their lives; children who have been supported through the difficult times in their lives are more likely to develop resilience.

To enable a child to develop self-control, he needs to experience the appropriate level of adult guidance and support. If a child experiences neglect or indifference he may become isolated, unsociable and unresponsive. The capacity to experience emotional status is the outcome of a secure attachment. The caregiver is able to tune into negative and positive states and the child can learn to do this in return.

Self-resilience is generated by social relatedness. A child who is anxiously attached, for example one whose carers did not respond to his need for reassurance and contact, can develop dependency problems later in life. A young baby cannot become 'spoiled' by receiving too much attention. Toddlers will consider all regular and positive experiences as being 'the norm' and will, through those experiences, learn how to behave towards other people in the future.

A child forms a strategy for coping with life as he finds it, and attempts to predict outcomes of actions and relationships based on early childhood experiences. This is carried on into adult life and is constantly evolving in the light of new experiences. While people can later effectively come to terms with adverse experiences, the effect of what they have encountered in the past will always be in the background.

Parent as we have been parented

Carers tend to bring up children in the same way that their own parents or carers brought them up. Even if their own experiences as a child were not pleasant, carers will naturally parent as they were parented without necessarily being aware of this. Carers who themselves in childhood experienced abuse or neglect (for example, where violent rows and harsh physical punishment were regular occurrences) may find it very difficult not to repeat this pattern of parenting themselves. Traumatic childhood memories may re-emerge in parenthood, causing carers to pass on to their own children the negative feelings engendered by these experiences. In turn, their children may then behave in the same way towards the next generation and so the cycle continues.

The cycle can be broken, and not everyone who has been abused will themselves become abusive. However, for those who do not resolve their problems, life is much less satisfying. Childhood experiences of neglect or abuse can result in the development of violent behaviours and the exhibition of such behaviours may have resulted from negative and damaging experiences in childhood.

How to encourage positive attachments

A nurturing, affectionate home environment and close physical contact with a carer are essential to help build attachment and to enable the child to grow into a well-rounded adult. Helping carers to bond with their baby in a fun, enjoyable and meaningful manner is the key. Practitioners can work directly with the carer and her baby in order to help them develop a positive attachment with each other. Early intervention is vital; therefore, encouraging carers to interact with their babies at an early stage is imperative for developing positive attachments. Babies need to feel loved, secure and nurtured in order to develop and grow.

Adults may forget, or never have learned, how to 'read' or understand their baby. However, practitioners can help caregivers to recognise, appreciate and enjoy their baby's achievements. Practitioners can also teach carers how to interact appropriately with their child through play-based experiences such as singing songs, copying actions, smiling and using positive praise, eye contact and a soft tone of voice. Practitioners can help the carer to notice how her child is responding and feeling. This should, in turn, give the carer the confidence to respond appropriately to her baby's needs. We want to provide opportunities for carers to build up a relationship of trust and respect. This can be done by encouraging both carer and practitioner to work together in partnership.

Insecure and indiscriminate attachments

Carers wishing to adopt or offer long-term foster care may be unsure about how to ensure that the baby in their care will learn to bond and form a secure attachment. As mentioned previously, babies need a secure and responsive carer in the first few months of life in order to form positive attachments. Initially babies may be indiscriminate in their search for affection (i.e. go to anyone for attention and care) but will then form a strong attachment to the new carer when they have learned to trust that person.

When the carer reads the baby's messages and signs, and responds appropriately, the baby will gradually realise that the new person in his life is reliable, consistent and sensitive to his needs. Trust will grow and the baby will start to turn to the new carer for help and comfort. He may then become anxious if an unfamiliar adult offers to take over his care, and look to the familiar carer for help. This is an encouraging sign. The baby seeks out his familiar carer and starts to show a dependency on the caring adult. The *Wiggle Giggle Hug and Tickle* programme is designed to help carers understand, approach and deal with the issues raised above.

Post-natal depression and attachment

Post-natal depression can make raising a baby very challenging. Being willing and able to meet the demands of a baby at any given moment can be a real struggle for the mother. If the mother is struggling to form a positive attachment with her child, this can affect her ability to tune into her baby's needs and respond promptly and appropriately. It is not enough to go through the motions of feeding, changing or even cuddling a baby in order to form a secure attachment. Mothers need to engage with their baby, have fun and read their baby's signals consistently in order for true bonding to occur. If the baby does not consistently have his needs met by his mother, this can lead to him having to learn how to self-soothe/self-regulate and can even lead to the baby becoming withdrawn and less responsive to the world and people around him.

Programmes designed to meet the needs of mothers with post-natal depression have been run in the Netherlands and Australia. Helping mothers with post-natal depression to bond and form a relationship with their baby has proven to be successful in developing positive attachments.

The *Wiggle Giggle Hug and Tickle* programme aims to address these very issues in a fun, friendly and non-judgemental way. It promotes nurturing behaviour and helps to develop a mother's skills and abilities in relation to reading and responding to her baby. Moreover, if the programme is run in a group format with a group of mothers experiencing the same, or similar, challenges, the group members can provide mutual support for each other.

Adoptive parents, foster carers and attachment

Babies and young pre-schoolers who are adopted or are going through the fostering process have often missed out, more than other babies, on the essential formative bonding experience.

This could be for many reasons such as poor early experiences of parenting, too many people handling them whilst waiting for an adoptive home, and turbulent, chaotic starts in life. Babies who have had a difficult start in life may also struggle to trust adults and can be reluctant to form a bond with someone. A baby may also have had negative attachment experiences such as 'My cries are not responded to so I may as well not bother' or 'The only time I'm held is when I cry so I'll cry more to get some attention.' Negative attachment experiences can make it extremely difficult for a foster carer or adoptive parent to develop secure attachments with that child; however, a positive attachment *can* be achieved. Happy, positive experiences between carer and baby can help to develop a healthy secure attachment between them even if the baby's previous experiences have not been so positive.[9]

The *Wiggle Giggle Hug and Tickle* programme addresses some of the stages in which a baby may have been deprived and will help the adoptive parent or foster carer not only to understand and read the signs the baby is giving but also to teach the carer to act appropriately.

· · · · · · · · · · · · ·

9   Furnival, J. [SIRCC, on behalf of Scottish Attachment in Action]. (2011) 'Attachment-informed practice with looked after children and young people.' Institute for Research and Innovation in Social Services (IRISS). *Insights, 10*. Available at www.iriss.org.uk/resources/attachment-informed-practice-looked-after-children-and-young-people, accessed on 28 April 2015.

2

Communication

Babies want to communicate

Babies are born into the world wanting to communicate. They can imitate facial expressions and gestures a few hours after being born. They will study faces, turn to sound and react to noises immediately. Early communication speeds up the acquisition of language and is associated with success in reading, writing and early social skills. Babies are amazingly receptive and intuitive. They absorb emotional tone, which is why adults usually speak to babies using a higher exaggerated pitch.

This is called 'mother-ese tongue'[10] and imitates a female voice, which is associated with comfort and food. Therefore, smile, look and respond. Try to decode what your baby is saying and imitate and mirror what he is doing. As well as copying him, remember to touch and use body language and stay physically connected.

Carers have to 'read' their child and tune in to positive/negative responses. What are they trying to tell you? To understand your baby's needs you must learn to recognise the non-verbal cues and body language. This will help ensure that your baby is happy, peaceful and content. If your baby is content then you are more likely to respond in a relaxed, calm and positive manner. Non-verbal communication is a two-way process. Baby and carer are watching each other: looking at each other's eyes, watching movements and trying to interpret facial expressions. A responsive gaze reassures your baby but a vacant expression can cause a baby to feel disturbed or anxious. When the baby is about three months old, signing can be introduced to reinforce the communicative bond.

Sign and gesture

What do we mean by sign and gesture? Imagine you are speaking to a person from another country (for example, a person from Italy, as Italians are well known for using gesture and gesticulation). Unable to understand the language, you may look perplexed and use gesture to communicate this, for example shaking your head, shrugging, making faces. In response, the person can use gesture to help express his meaning, for example pointing. Similarly, when communicating with babies, supplementing the spoken word with sign and gesture aids understanding. In addition to this, research has shown that the use of sign and gesture can help to develop spoken language. A baby who

10 'Mother-ese tongue is a style of speech involving rate, pitch, simplicity and physical distance.' Cooper, R. P. and Aislin, R. N. (1994) 'Developmental Differences in Infant Attention to the Spectral Properties of Infant-Directed Speech.' *Child Development*, 65, 6, 1663–1677.

experiences and uses gestures in the first 14 months of his life is more likely to develop a wider vocabulary. [11]

The acquisition of speech and being able to express oneself can also reduce tantrums and frustration (for both carer and baby). The use of gesture and sign thus aids understanding and enables a baby to communicate at an earlier stage in life than the use of spoken language alone. Siblings in the family may feel more included as they can also use the signs. Research agrees that the carers who do use gesture are more responsive and sensitive to their baby's non-verbal cues and it encourages them to think of their baby as an individual.

Carers can be worried that the use of sign might inhibit their baby from talking. This is not the case and in fact the reverse is true. Signing promotes the development of early language, as long the sign is used at the same time as the word. The sign should always be accompanied by the key word and never used in isolation. Babies can relatively quickly and easily begin to copy simple signs (such as juice, milk, biscuit) and use these signs independently to express their needs. Babies can control their hands more easily than their vocal cords. At around 8–12 months they can wave goodbye, point, and shake their head for 'no'. They learn by watching. If you say 'I love you' it may mean something, but a loving gesture means so much more. Signing supports communication and expresses emotion.

Many basic signs are 'common sense' and are probably very similar to signs and gestures one would use in everyday communication. The signs are taught in a developmental order and, as they are meaningful, babies respond with enthusiasm. It is advisable to begin with one or two simple signs then add more gradually. The introduction of too many different signs in the early stages will be confusing and off-putting for the baby. Most importantly, ensure that the sign being used is consistent and that everyone who is signing to the baby uses the same sign.

Description of signs

As long as you are consistent, and use the same signs every time, it does not really matter which signs you use. However, the word must be said at the same time as the sign is performed. On the following page is a description of how to perform each sign and we have also included photographs of some of the signs on page 28. You can visit www.jkp.com/catalogue/book/9781849056564 to view videos of the signs being demonstrated.

11 Kirk, E., Howlett, N., Pine, K. J., and Fletcher, B. C. (2012) 'To sign or not to sign? The impact of encouraging infants to gesture on infant language and maternal mind-mindedness.' *Child Development*, 84, 2, 574–590.

Again/repeat	Open scissor fingers. Strike down.
Cuddle	Cross arms over your chest. Place hands touching opposite shoulders and give yourself a squeeze.
Daddy	Palms down, place index and middle fingers of one hand on top of index and middle fingers of other hand. Tap twice.
Finished	Place both hands face down in midline. Cross one hand over other then move hands away from each other.
Friend	Shake your own hand.
Goodbye	Wave goodbye.
Hat	Use two hands to imitate pulling on a hat on your own head.
Hello	Thumb-up sign then move wrist side-to-side.
Home/house	Touch two flat hands at fingertips to make a roof shape.
Love	Place two hands over your heart.
More	Pretend to hold a cup handle with one hand then place other hand flat on top.
Mummy	Use index, middle and ring fingers to tap twice on other palm.
Peek-a-boo	Place two flat hands in front of own eyes then slide hands away to either side.
Play	Make a fist with both hands, extend thumb and pinkie (little finger) then shake wrists.
Please	Place flat hand on own chin and move hand in a downward arc away from chin.
Sit down	Place one flat hand on top of the other flat hand then push both hands down.
Thank you	Place flat hand on own chin and move hand a few inches forward from chin.
Tickle	Wiggle all your fingers.
Wait	Place hands flat and facing downwards with fingers pointing towards each other. Place one hand on top of other and roll hands backwards in circular motion.
Well done/Good/Great	Thumb up.

Again/Repeat

Cuddle

Daddy

Finished

Friend

Please

Peek-a-boo (1)

Peek-a-boo (2)

Wait

Some basic signs

Rhyme and song

Music is fundamental to early literacy development. Singing to our children can be soothing and calming (for example, 'Rock-a-bye baby') but can also raise spirits and be exciting (for example, 'Humpty Dumpty sat on a wall'). Listening to and learning songs helps to develop vocabulary. Rhythm is part of life and it is never too early to introduce it to our children. Nursery rhymes are a good way to start and it is not necessary to be able to sing in tune as the rhythm and actions are the most important ingredients. Babies love the rhythm and pattern of song and it helps them to learn language. Adding words to music and rhythm helps the brain to learn quickly and retain what it has learned.

Research has been carried out on premature babies exposed to music for 40-minute sessions over a period of four days. It demonstrated that those babies who were exposed to the music gained more weight, had lower blood pressure and had a stronger heartbeat compared with a control group.[12]

Babies respond to rhythm and singing and therefore exposure to music and rhythm is an important foundation in a baby's development. The ear is the first organ to develop in the womb and, as early as five months gestation, a baby can hear and respond to music. It has been suggested that babies up to a year old can remember the tunes to which they were exposed in the womb.[13]

Whilst singing nursery rhymes we are likely, even unconsciously, to bounce babies up and down and do the actions. These movements stimulate the reflexes that are so necessary for survival, that is, the flight and fight responses, the saving reflexes and protective reactions.

The tunes and words may be simple and repetitive, but therein lies their value. Babies can discriminate music from speech and do not judge performance. Turn off the TV and switch on the stereo. Dance together and create a love of music in your child. It is a wonderful way to bond and encourage language development at the same time.

· · · · · · · · · · · · · ·

12 Stanley, J. (1991) 'The Role of Music in Pacification/Stimulation of Premature Infants of Low Birthweights.' *Music Therapy Perspectives*, 9, 1, 19–25.
Lorch, C. A., Lorch, V., Diefendorf, A. O., Earl, P. W. (1994) 'The Effects of Stimulative and Sedative Music on Systolic Blood Pressure, Heart Rate and Respiratory Rate in Premature Infants.' *The Journal of Music Therapy*, 31, 2, 105–118.

13 Partanen, E. Kujala, T., Tervaniemi, M., Huotilaninen, M. (2013) 'Prenatal Music Exposure Induces Long Term Neural Effects.' *PLoS One*. 30 October 2013, DOI: 10.1371/journal.pone.0078946.

Action songs can be initiated from the early days of a baby's life. These songs and rhymes help to develop not only language, but also numeracy, body awareness and social interaction.

We have discussed why babies benefit from music, but why do babies like singing with their carer? Babies like the sound of the words, the rhythm, and the anticipation of familiar parts of the song, the movement and the actions. They respond to the facial expression, the one-to-one interaction, and the physical closeness of the carer. Music and rhythm are fun and 'made-up' songs to suit a particular occasion are as valuable as well-known songs or rhymes. There are many different types of tunes and singing games that you can use, such as bouncing rhymes, finger rhymes and action songs.

3

Movement

The importance of movement

Children love to move. It is by moving through their environment that a child can change a two-dimensional image into a three-dimensional image. A child will learn about spatial relationships, can judge distance and depth and will have a better understanding of where their own body is in the world just by moving around in it.

When children are very small and unable to move from one place to another independently, it is the job of the adult to provide the different movement opportunities that the baby craves. One very successful movement is rocking. This can be very soothing for the child or it can be made to be exciting and stimulating. Bouncing is another movement that can be used in play activities or to help distract a child, for example when he becomes upset.

If children are not used to exploring their environment, they will not try to or they might even become fearful of it. If the fear of movement is overcome they are more able to explore the world and develop as confident individuals. We are actively encouraging babies to experience different types of movement and balance activities in order to develop the necessary reflexes required in life. When babies move, they often need help, for example to roll, sit, stand or walk. In order to help them we use touch, which naturally releases endorphins, the 'feel-good' hormones in our brain.

As a baby moves, he begins to learn about himself and the world around him. He can explore the environment and learn where he is within that environment. Movement also allows a baby to develop muscle strength and coordination; that is, how to move his arms and legs in a purposeful and controlled manner.

There are two halves to our brain, a right side and a left side. Each half controls movements to the other side of the body; that is, the left side of the brain moves the right side of the body and vice versa. It is important that both halves of the brain are used in order to have good overall body movements.

Tummy time

Nowadays, carers are advised to place babies on their backs to sleep. Babies are also placed in bouncy cradles, buggies, prams and activity play mats on their back. Therefore, many babies are often being denied the chance to lie on their tummies. As a result, they tend to dislike lying or being placed on their tummies as it is unfamiliar to them and can be an effort to maintain this position initially. This can mean that they are not getting much opportunity to learn physical skills that are vital for typical physical development; for example, the baby may be slow to roll or crawl. Reflexes that a baby would naturally develop are being restricted and inhibited.

Moreover, if babies lie on their backs too much, they can develop an uneven head shape. A prominent flattening of the back of the skull is called plagiocephaly, which can be difficult to correct as babies grow and their skulls become tougher. (In some cases, babies are issued with helmets to reshape their skulls.)

Children who do not experience tummy time can also have delayed head and back extension, and poor shoulder stability, as they have not used their arms to push their body up off the ground (such skills are all required for crawling). Pushing up on the hands also helps to define the arches and smaller muscles within a baby's hand, which are essential for engaging in hand function activities later on in life, for example holding a pencil and using cutlery. Sighted children are motivated to turn their heads to see what is happening, but because of current trends of lying babies on their backs to sleep, they are slower to lift their heads than babies born 20 years ago (when babies were placed on their sides or tummies).

Reflexes

When babies are born, they display various movements that they cannot control. These automatic movements are called reflexes, which start to develop as early as when a baby is in the womb. Babies practise all of these reflexes until they can achieve them without thinking. Some of these reflexes you 'use and lose', for example the grasp reflex, and some you 'gain and retain', for example the startle reflex. All reflexes are important for learning, development and survival. On the next page are some of the reflexes found in babies. It is important to remember that the reflexes are very dependent on how a baby is feeling at that time.

Reflexes	What happens?	Why is it needed?	What if it is not present?	'Use and lose' or 'gain and retain'?
Rooting	Baby turns head if cheek is touched	To find the nipple for feeding	Difficulty feeding and gaining weight	Use and lose
Hand grasp	Hand will grasp a finger when placed in baby's palm	Teaches baby to grip and teaches hand awareness	Problems in using hands, possible writing problems later on in life	Use and lose
Foot grasp	Toes will curl around a finger when placed just under baby's toes	Preparation for walking and helps to develop balance	Difficulty walking, poor foot skills	Use and lose
Balance	Maintains an upright posture when sitting independently	For safety, balance and coordination	Fear of sitting unsuported	Gain and retain
Startle	Sudden noise makes baby's arms move outwards then into body	To try and defend himself	Distracted, always alert, concentration may be poor	Gain and retain
Asymmetric Tonic Neck Reflex	Turns head to one side to see extended arm, whilst other arm will bend at elbow	Helps baby to roll to side, develops hand–eye coordination, starts to kick	Poor middle skills. May neglect other side of body	Use and lose
Symmetric Tonic Neck Reflex	Arms bend as head goes down, then arms straighten as head goes up	Preparation for rocking then crawling, gives strength against gravity	Poor ball skills and balance	Use and lose

Positions for play

It is important that children experience a wide variety of different positions in which to play. This helps them to strengthen and coordinate different muscle groups at different times and also provides them with different fun, rewarding experiences. Below are various playing positions and why they are important.

LYING ON YOUR BACK

Physical development	Strengthens neck, tummy, shoulder and hip flexors as children have to lift head, arms and legs up against gravity.
Cognitive development	It is the first stage in the awareness of cause-and-effect play. For example, if I hit something such as a dangling toy, it moves or makes a sound.
Sensory development	This is the position in which it is easiest for children to focus their eyes on a person or object or track a moving object.

LYING ON YOUR TUMMY

Physical development	Strengthens neck and back as child brings head up against gravity. Pushing up through forearm or hands also develops strong shoulder muscles in preparation to crawl. It is also an important foundation for the transition to sitting.
Cognitive development	The child sees their environment from a different perspective and explores what their body is capable of in order to move or play in this position.
Sensory development	The child experiences the sensation of lying on their tummy as opposed to on their back.

LYING ON YOUR SIDE

Physical development	This position encourages the hands to come together in the child's midline, therefore two-handed play can develop. The child also contracts their muscles to balance in order to maintain this position.
Cognitive development	Hands and eyes start to learn to work together, and spatial awareness begins to emerge.
Sensory development	The ability to use their hands together more freely enables children to explore a wider variety of textures, shapes and sizes.

SITTING ON THE FLOOR

Physical development	Stabilises the pelvis and trunk, allowing the arms and hands to be free. Enabling learning to maintain an upright, balanced posture against gravity whilst also learning to use their hands to save themselves if they fall to the side.
Cognitive development	Enables children to realise that when upright, their world is three-dimensional.
Sensory development	The ability to use their hands more freely enables children to explore a wider variety of textures, shapes and sizes.

ON HANDS AND KNEES

Physical development	Children are supporting their body weight against gravity, strengthening muscles which may be used for other movements later on. It also enables the child to move freely and independantly around their environment independently by crawling.
Cognitive development	Helps children to understand the relationship between their body and their environment, known as spatial awareness.
Sensory development	Encourages weight-bearing through extended arms and open palms.

STANDING

Physical development	Children are supporting their body weight against gravity, strengthening muscles around their hips and ankles which may be used for other gross motor movements later on, for example running, climbing, and jumping.
Cognitive development	Allows children to be independent in exploring and learning about their environment.
Sensory development	Children gain greater understanding of their environment and how their body relates to objects and other people within that environment.

4

Sensory

Sensory processing

Every day, we absorb a great variety of different sensory information from around us in just a split second; what we see, hear, smell and touch. Our brain processes the sensory information so that we can make sense of the world in which we live. We have seven senses which we use to gather information from the world: sight, sound, smell, taste, touch, balance and body awareness.

Our senses begin to function very early in life but we often use them unconsciously (think of a baby and how he needs to suck, smell, be rocked and be cradled). The senses work together in an integrated and automatic way. This happens most importantly in the first five years of a child's life.

Sensory processing is the name given to the process whereby the brain gives meaning to the sensations that it receives from the environment and enables us to make sense of the world. Without the ability to process and understand sensory information, the world can be a frightening and confusing place.

If children have difficulty processing sensory information they may display symptoms such as:

- avoidance of touching certain textures

- a need to touch/carry a certain comfort object

- sensitivity or abnormal response to light and sounds

- high activity levels and a tendency to seek out movement

- poor or delayed development of movement skills

- poor concentration and attention to tasks

- difficulty settling to sleep.

These sensory processing experiences may involve the child reacting in different ways; either by avoiding a particular sense (because they feel it is too much sensory information for the brain to process so they try to avoid it) or by seeking more of a particular sense (because they feel that there is not enough sensory information for the brain to process so they need more).

As adults, environmental stimulation can either alert us or calm us. For example, we might drink coffee to keep us awake, or we might listen to soft music to relax us. Moreover, the same stimulation might alert one person, but calm another; for example, chewing gum can help calm us when we are anxious or keep us alert when we are tired. As adults, we know what we can do to help us remain alert or to help calm us down. However, babies cannot understand these feelings on their own and rely on their carers to know what they need and when. Children will require different calming or alerting experiences throughout their day.

Listed below are the seven senses with examples of some seeking and avoiding reactions you may see in a child.

SIGHT

- *Avoidance*: Dislike of bright lights; tendency to look down.

- *Seeking*: Attracted to light; fascinated with reflections; looks intently at objects; moves fingers/objects in front of eyes.

SOUND

- *Avoidance*: Covers ears; light sleeper; dislikes sudden noises or loud noises; may make repetitive noise to block out other sounds.

- *Seeking*: Bangs objects; seeks noisy environment; makes loud, rhythmic noises.

SMELL

- *Avoidance*: Avoids smell; may avoid some people due to perfume, for example; often has toileting problems.

- *Seeking*: Smells objects; seeks strong odours; bed-wetting.

TASTE

- *Avoidance*: Poor eater; uses tip of tongue for testing; gags/vomits easily.

- *Seeking*: Eats anything; seeks strong flavours; puts objects in the mouth or licks them.

TOUCH

- *Avoidance*: Resists being touched; difficulty tolerating new clothes; avoids certain textures and certain foods; over-reacts to heat, cold and pain; avoids messy play; avoids haircuts and hairwashing, brushing teeth, nail-cutting, bathing; may appear irritable or fearful when others are close, for example lining up to go into class.

- *Seeking*: Seeks deep pressure; hugs tightly; prone to self-injury, for example head-banging, biting self; low reaction to pain and temperature; appears unaware of touch unless very intense; unaware of messiness, for example a runny nose; may hurt others without realising the impact it has on them; may have difficulty performing certain motor tasks without visual cues, for example writing; difficulty holding objects, for example pencil, fork.

BALANCE

- *Avoidance*: Fearful reactions to ordinary movements or activities; difficulty walking on uneven surfaces; dislikes being upside down or rough and tumble; intolerant of movement; dislikes moving platforms, for example escalators; suffers from car sickness.

- *Seeking*: Seeks very intense sensory experiences such as spinning, rocking, jumping, flapping hands, bouncing on furniture, lying upside down on furniture; calms with movement stimulation.

BODY AWARENESS

- *Avoidance*: Difficulty manipulating objects; turns whole body to look at something; difficulty going up/down stairs; heavy pencil work; a tendency to break toys.

- *Seeking*: Low muscle tone; weak grip; lacks awareness of body positions; likes to be tucked tightly in cot; likes to have clothes tucked in.

Intervention

Children should be encouraged to gradually use all of their senses in order to overcome any fears of sensory stimulation in the future. They should be guided through activities that challenge their ability to respond appropriately to sensory input. Gentle, graded exposure to avoidance-type behaviours can help a child to increase gradually their tolerance to a particular sensation. Children who seek more of a particular sensation can be provided with additional input in a safe and controlled manner. The *Wiggle Giggle Hug and Tickle* programme primarily focuses on movement, touch and body-awareness senses.

Body awareness

Just as our eyes and ears send information to the brain about what we see and hear, parts of our muscles and joints sense the position of our body and also send these messages to the brain. We depend on this information to know exactly where our body parts are and what movement they are making. We need this information to plan other movements.

Children who have a poor sense of body awareness may be uncoordinated or clumsy, may bump into things or generally find it difficult to manage themselves in the most efficient manner.

This sense helps us to manage everyday functions in life such as: staying in a comfortable position in a chair; holding utensils properly (such as a pen or a fork); judging how to move through space so that we do not run into things; planning how much pressure to apply so that we do not break a pencil lead or a toy; changing actions that were not successful at first attempts, for example throwing a ball that was off target.

Problems in this system can cause a great deal of difficulty for the child and, as a result, he has to pay attention to actions that should happen automatically. The child may feel clumsy, frustrated and even fearful in some situations. For example, it may be very scary to walk downstairs if you are not sure where your feet are in relation to the rest of your body and the stairs being negotiated.

Balance

The balance system lets us know where we are in the world. It lets us know which way up we are and in which direction we are moving. It also lets us know how fast we are moving.

A sense of balance acts as a warning to alert us if we are about to overbalance or fall. It allows us to register that our feet are placed firmly on the ground, giving us a sense of safety, and helps us adjust our body position in order to maintain the 'just right' posture for any given task.

Children may have problems maintaining balance and using their two hands together if they have difficulties in this area.

Some children with balance difficulties may move more than other children in order to get a sense of where they are and what they are doing. They need the movement in order to focus and help them to listen and understand.

Touch

The tactile system is responsible for our sense of touch. As a baby, it is one of the first sensory systems from which we receive information. It tells us about the world around us and helps us to feel safe and secure. It is one of the most important senses we use and is vital when developing a bond with another person. Touch can also be calming, reassuring and enjoyable.

5

Play

The importance of play

It is well recognised that play is a vital part of a child's life, and children love to play. However, for children, playing is so much more than just having fun. It is how they learn about the world around them. Play allows a child to try out new experiences and practise behaviours without worrying about the consequences. It develops cognition, coordination, imagination, social skills and speech by utilising the seven senses that are explained in Chapter 4.

Different forms of play include, for example, with objects, imaginary play, with another person, solitary play, sedentary tasks, and rough and tumble. Play time is more than just using toys or equipment. Babies love, and benefit greatly from, playful interaction with their carer such as singing, action/finger rhymes and playing peek-a-boo and tickling games. Such play activities, enjoyed in a warm, affectionate environment, will allow children to develop and thrive.

Baby play

When babies are first born, they are ready and willing to learn. Play may involve babies tracking an object passing in front of their eyes, grasping a soft toy or being sung to and swayed from side to side. As babies get older, their play becomes more complex and explorative. Babies are intrigued by objects; they want to know what they are and what they do. Mouthing objects is a key method used by babies to explore various concepts such as the texture and weight of that object. Movement helps to transform the world from a two-dimensional into a three-dimensional world. The baby learns how to move within the environment which, in turn, teaches the baby about judging depth and distance. Movement also activates important muscle groups that are required for balance and strength. Play helps with communication as, when they hear the words used by an adult in a play activity, the child attempts to copy and practise these sounds.

The carer's role in play

The carer has the key role in assisting the baby to play as she is the one who provides the opportunities to create and shape play experiences according to the needs of her baby. The carer will initiate play activities and include the child in the play (for example, by singing or talking to her baby, moving her baby around in a game). The carer can guide the play in an appropriate direction and adapt the content of the play according to the baby's reactions and responses.

Playing with her baby also gives the carer a chance to learn how to play as she did herself when she was young, and to find that child-like inner self. If the baby is having fun then the carer will most likely be having fun too.

When a carer plays with her baby, and is able to make the two-way play process fun, the baby is learning social skills such as sharing and turn-taking. These are vital everyday skills that we use as adults to interact appropriately with others in a variety of different situations. Play helps a baby to develop social and emotional skills as he feels loved and important to someone who is the centre of his world. Developing a close relationship with his carer, through play, helps a baby to develop feelings of self-worth and self-respect. This, in turn, can build the baby's self-confidence, which is an important quality to enable the child to be able to develop and sustain loving, supportive and healthy relationships in adulthood.

Signs of readiness to play

It is important to be able to tune in to the child's reactions and responses to play. Carers should soon learn to gauge whether the baby is enjoying the play and wants it to continue, or has had enough and would like it to end. Being aware of body signals is the most effective way of knowing what your baby wants. For example, a baby may want the activity to continue if he reaches out his hands for an object, if he maintains eye contact, if he smiles, laughs, flaps his hands or squeals in delight. Your baby may have had enough if he looks away, frowns, cries or ignores an object offered to him. A carer has to follow her baby's lead and ensure that she does not insist on continuing an activity if the baby is reluctant to engage with her.

Every child has the right to play. If a child is denied the opportunity to play he will have difficulty developing into a well-rounded adult. Play allows children to express their feelings and show emotions. It allows them to grow and develop at their own pace and is an integral component of holistic development.

Responsive play

There is a time and a place for structured play activities; however, children should also be allowed the freedom to choose their play, rather than play opportunities always being guided or controlled by an adult.

There should be time for play to be self-motivated and freely chosen. We should not, as adults, impose our values on the child because, by doing that, we change the very nature of play. This does not mean that adults should not get involved in children's play and share the experience; just as long as the play is not always adult-directed. Being 'child-led' means that the adult follows the child and respects the child's lead. As adults, we should not always take the lead role in directing play or conversation, nor should we hurry children. Naturally, of course, there are some boundaries and limits to be set but, overall, it is best to, when appropriate, follow the child rather than always expect them to follow us. We can offer toys, games, stories, and so on, but try to be responsive to the child's reaction. Stop if they turn away or ignore the toy or game. Offer an alternative activity or redirect the child's gaze and attention to something else. There is a balance between supporting play (offering opportunities) and dominating play (being overly directive). We as adults must be in tune with the child's play and respect their play choices. It is too easy and tempting to take over a child's game, for example by giving too much help.

This advice equally applies to babies. A baby will provide you with clues if you pay attention to his body movements, facial expressions and vocalisations. Follow a baby's lead and build on the relationship by responding appropriately. It can be very simple and repetitive but if you look at your baby, and engage with him closely, you will soon tune in to what he needs and wants. Does he want the activity again/repeated? Is he keen to continue with the activity or has he lost interest?

A loving, strong and understanding attachment will continue to grow and develop as the carer plays and interacts with her child. If her child loses interest, is it because he has become bored with the game, or perhaps because he is hungry or tired? The carer will learn through practice, patience and repetition.

6

Child Development (0–2 Years)

Milestones in child development

As children grow and develop, they ideally attain certain milestones and follow a sequence of developmental stages, within an approximate time scale. It is important that practitioners working with young children are knowledgeable about child development. However, it is essential to recognise that children are unique individuals and they will develop at their own pace and in their own time.

The general guide listed on the next page is a reference tool, and should not be used to determine exactly what a specific child can, or cannot, do at a specific age. We do not want to cause unnecessary anxiety if a child does not acquire a particular skill at a particular age. Careful observation, liaising with the carers and good communication with others involved, should be paramount when trying to determine a particular child's abilities. Children may perform better on some days than on others as certain factors may hinder their performance, for example anxiety, illness or lethargy. There are numerous factors that can delay a child's development, including physical or learning impairment, and social factors such as abuse, neglect and negative attachments with caregivers. However, understanding the typical pattern of child development will help to assess whether a child is thriving or struggling in any given situation. This knowledge will also help to determine the performance areas in which a child may require further assistance. It may also help to promote the child's development in each skill area.

This guide for appropriate age development is not an extensive list. A selection of skills is listed for each area of development. The areas of development have been broken down into five different categories; Cognitive, Emotional, Physical, Play and Sensory.

By 6 months old, children may:

Cognitive	Imitate sounds and enjoy babbling, be interested in others but wary of strangers, hold hands up awaiting to be held, recognise familiar people's voices, cry/scream to get adult attention.
Emotional	Use body movements to express pleasure, for example when being fed or bathed, enjoy cuddling, attention and listening to voices, imitate facial expressions, smile in response to an adult, find sucking action calming, be wary of strangers, become upset when carer leaves.
Physical	Roll over from back to tummy, lift head and chest up off ground when lying on tummy, bear almost all of their own weight, sit with hands being held by an adult, poke at objects with their finger.
Play	Use hands to touch, stroke and pat objects, pass a toy from one hand to another, reach out to grab a toy when offered, like being rocked and bounced, enjoy rhythm and songs, for example listening to singing.
Sensory	Focus on objects less than 1 metre away, recognise their mother's voice, take objects to mouth, be visually alert and watch people and objects moving around a room, turn head towards sounds.

By 1 year old, children may:

Cognitive	Look for a hidden toy, recognise familiar pictures, for example family members, understand 'no' and 'bye bye', imitate adult noises, for example brrrr or a cough, babble loudly and continuously.
Emotional	Like a comfort object, for example a blanket or teddy, feel secure if they can see a familiar adult.
Physical	Sit, crawl, bottom shuffle, rise to standing without assistance, stand holding on to furniture, pick up small objects, pass toys from one hand to the other, maintain hold of an object, for example a rattle or piece of toast, possibly walk independently.
Play	Make noises by banging objects, place toys into and out of boxes, play with stacking beakers and bricks, explore objects with hands and mouth, enjoy rough and tumble, play alone for long periods.
Sensory	Turn to the sound of their carer's voice or a sudden noise, mouth objects to explore them, use a comforter such as a dummy/ pacifier, be very visually alert to their surroundings.

By 18 months old, children may:

Cognitive	Point to known objects and body parts on request, use several words and understand many more, imitate words that an adult says, use gestures, for example wave hands, follow stories, remember where objects belong.
Emotional	Play contently alone, display a desire to be independent, become frustrated, have occasional tantrums.
Physical	Walk steadily and stop safely, climb forward into an adult chair and sit down, kneel upright without support, squat to pick up a toy, climb stairs with adult assistance.
Play	Build a tower with a few bricks, scribble with a crayon, explore and manipulate objects, display a desire to be independent, enjoy playing with paints and crayons, enjoy puppet play, action games, pop-up toys, balls and stacking toys.
Sensory	Recognise people at a distance, recognise their own reflection in a mirror, enjoy exploring sand, play dough and water, explore different shapes, sizes and weights of objects.

By 2 years old, children may:

Cognitive	Understand basic instructions, for example kiss Mummy, show interest in picture books, begin to show empathy, begin to join up two words, name objects, express feelings.
Emotional	Try out new experiences eagerly, begin to express how they feel but also become frustrated when attempts are not understood or carried out by others, be impulsive and curious, be very emotionally dependent on an adult.
Physical	Run safely, avoiding obstacles, climb up onto furniture, throw a ball overhand, walk up and down stairs, jump with both feet together, kick a large ball, use a spoon, draw lines, circles and dots on paper, dress some of self, drink from a cup.
Play	Play with posting boxes and shape sorters, screw/unscrew objects, enjoy puppet and action games, begin to engage in imaginative play, for example put dolly to bed, tolerate others playing beside them, enjoy picture books, turn pages of book.
Sensory	Recognise familiar people in photographs, listen to conversations with interest, show curiosity about their environment.

Developmental delay

Children with developmental delay may have a specific learning difficulty or a diagnosis such as Down syndrome. However, some children may not have an obvious disability but may have general social, emotional, physical or behavioural difficulties at various levels of severity. Many children have no specific diagnosis and there may be no clear explanation as to why the child is not functioning at the same level as his peers.

There are many standardised tests that can be completed to determine if a child is developmentally delayed. Often, this is an inconsistent profile (by this we mean that a child may score well in some areas but not in others).

As children grow and develop, they need to be exposed to a range of different experiences. What they see, hear and play with are all vital contributory factors in their development. Children with developmental delay may require more frequent and intense input or intervention compared with other children of a similar age. Alternatively, children with developmental delay may have missed experiential opportunities, for example due to family circumstances such as poverty and neglect. It is not too late to offer children an experience when they get a little bit older. A child with developmental delay often requires repetition and routine in order to learn new developmental skills. We believe that the *Wiggle Giggle Hug and Tickle* programme provides such an opportunity.

Children learn by seeing and doing, which is why they benefit greatly from interacting with their peers in a fun activity. However, many children with developmental delay are isolated in their play and they may need support to enable them to interact with others. Children with developmental delay may prefer, initially, to be a casual observer but it is important that they become active participants as soon as possible. Adult assistance can facilitate this process to ensure that the child can freely experience the activities on offer. A key strategy to enable the child to participate willingly is to make the activity motivational and tailored to his individual preferences. If the child enjoys what is happening, he will want to do it again and again.

As adults, we can offer activities that will enhance a child's play and ensure that the activity is adapted to meet the specific need of the child. We can offer support to a child and ensure that activities are gauged at an appropriate level. It is also important to offer praise and encouragement which, in turn, should develop a child's confidence and self-worth, as well as the ability to carry out daily activities. As soon as it is suspected that a child may be reaching milestones at a slower rate than expected, it is imperative that the child is offered multiple opportunities to promote his sense of self-confidence. It is important that children experience activities that they may have missed out on in order to help them reach their full potential. This should encompass play, posture, exposure to the senses and movement opportunities.

As children may not be able to tell you verbally how they are feeling, careful observation is essential. Look closely at a child's facial expressions and reactions to give you an idea of how to respond.

Adults should accompany spoken words with signs, gestures and exaggerated facial expressions. (As mentioned previously, think of how gesture helps if you are in a foreign country and speak not a word of the language.) Similarly, children who are struggling to understand what you are asking or saying benefit greatly from the use of non-verbal cues. Gesture and other visual cues reinforce the verbal word, thus enabling the child to understand more easily what is being asked, or said.

Developmental age vs developmental stage

It is appropriate to consider the stage at which the child is functioning, rather than the actual age of the child. This is particularly true for a child who has had a stormy start in life. For example, a child may be 3 years old but be presenting at the approximate age of a 1-year-old. The programme would be appropriate and, it is hoped, very enjoyable for this child.

Children often go through certain types of age-related behaviour, for example temper tantrums, when a child around the age of two can exhibit defiant and strong-willed behaviour. This is often referred to as 'the terrible twos'. However, if the child has a developmental delay, age-related behaviours are more likely to occur when the child is older. It is to be hoped that children who have a delay in their development will eventually reach the 'typical' developmental milestones expected of them, albeit at a considerably slower rate. The activities offered in this programme are suitable for children from around a developmental age of 2 months to 2 years.

Physical or learning disability

A child who has a physical or cognitive disability may not necessarily follow the typical developmental milestones. A child may meet some developmental stages on target but not others. Some children may achieve milestones later than expected and some may never attain some developmental milestones.

This should be taken into consideration when determining the developmental stage of each child.

Children with additional difficulties may require more time, and extra support, in order to complete certain activities or learn new skills. Other factors may affect the development of a child with a physical or cognitive difficulty, such as the learning opportunities to which they are exposed. Children with additional support needs will require additional help. Although children with impairments have the same basic needs as 'typically' developing children, a child with a disability can often miss out on essential opportunities and experiences. This can have a negative effect on the child forming relationships with others, learning new skills and engaging in physical, developmental and sensory activities.

Emotional immaturity

As stated previously, children reach developmental milestones at their own pace, such as the rate at which a child's emotional maturity develops. Securely attached babies learn how to calm down when upset and to communicate to another person that they need help or are becoming distressed. When a baby learns that his needs will be met in a consistent manner, he learns about positive social relationships (I cry, mummy cuddles me; I smile, mummy smiles back; I don't want to play just now, mummy stops the game).

However, a child who has not formed a secure attachment may not be equipped with the social skills required to interact with others as he grows older. Babies who do not form a secure attachment may become stressed more readily. They may develop unwanted social behaviours because they have not learned how to control their emotions and communicate in a more effective manner. For example, an insecurely attached child who is confronted with a social dilemma at a playgroup may have frequent tantrum outbursts or struggle to calm down when upset. He may over-react in certain situations, struggle to share toys, have difficulty being patient and lack empathy. A lack of ability to self-regulate and interact with others in a socially acceptable manner can make learning and forming relationships challenging. It would be developmentally acceptable for a young child to display many of the behaviours described above. However, should the child continue to display this behaviour for a prolonged period, this would suggest an emotional immaturity. It is becoming increasingly common to assess a child's emotional readiness to start school, rather than merely focusing on a child's academic readiness to start school.

7

Supporting Carers

The *Wiggle Giggle Hug and Tickle* programme helps carers to interact with their child in a fun, rewarding and delightful way in order to help strengthen the bond between one another. This book will assist the professional to support the carer to provide her baby with singing, movement and sensory experiences within the home environment.

The programme is a practical resource that will benefit any carer wanting to strengthen that carer/baby bond, and will be particularly useful for foster carers, adoptive parents, and mothers with post-natal depression and other mental health issues, who may require additional support to develop relationship and interaction skills with their baby. The required materials are inexpensive and easy to source. The songs mentioned throughout the book are well known and can be found via the web link.

The carer may prefer to carry out the suggested activities in a one-to-one manner in order to build up a two-way trust. This method is especially good for new adoptive parents or foster carers who may, at the early stage, want to build on a stronger attachment with the baby before introducing him to other, unfamiliar people.

Be consistent and follow a routine

When a child has come to live in a new home, everything is unfamiliar to him; the different smells, faces, voices and routines can be extremely distressing and overwhelming. The child's protective, survival mode will tell him to view unfamiliar experiences as a potential threat until he knows otherwise. Therefore, in the early stages at least, it is imperative that a predictable routine is followed.

When the child has learned that he can predict what is about to happen (and that the activity is of no threat to him) then he can relax and enjoy the playful experience. When the child also realises that the carer is a constant, predictable person, who is encouraging him to engage in enjoyable activities, he can start to develop a trusting, secure attachment with that person.

Be prepared

Be ready for the programme in advance by ensuring that the carer has all the required activities and materials prepared prior to starting each session. The carer should play in the same room and set the room up before beginning the first activity to ensure that the session runs smoothly.

Although the sessions follow a routine, it is the carer's responsibility to choose the activities that will be undertaken throughout the session. Use the

Session Planner (see the Appendix, page 77) to fill in the blanks for each session. Suggested songs and activities are also listed in the book, and audio tracks and videos can be found online at: www.jkp.com/catalogue/book/9781849056564. The times stated on the Session Planner are a guide as to how long the carer should spend on each activity.

Session structure

A. 'WIGGLE GIGGLE' SONG

The carer should start the play session with this song in order to signify to her baby that the play session is about to start. It should help her baby to settle and focus. The carer should sit face to face with her child on her knee to promote interaction and eye contact.

B. 'HELLO' SONG

Next is the 'Hello' song. Using a hat, this song encourages interaction, sharing and letting go of an object when asked to. The song can be repeated as many times as is liked. Any hat can be used but use the same hat in each session. A hat with bright colours or bells will be more fascinating to a young baby. Wearing an eye-catching hat also helps the child look up to see his carer's face. This is a particularly good time for the carer to smile and make funny faces while she has her child's attention.

C. NURSERY RHYMES

Nursery rhymes encourage a carer to sing to her child. Babies love melodic, repetitive sounds and singing and nursery rhymes are perfect for this. As the sessions progress, the carer will get to know which nursery rhymes her child likes best. Encourage the carer to be animated when singing and to perform the actions that accompany the song (make them up if you don't know them). The more the carer sings, the less she might feel 'silly' about singing.

When the song has ended, the carer is to ask her baby if he would like to hear the nursery rhyme again. The carer should look out for non-verbal cues that her child is saying 'yes' (eye contact, reaching out with hands, flapping hands, making vocal noises). The nursery rhyme is then sung again. If her baby looks away, cries, or appears generally disinterested, this may be the child's way of saying 'no' to hearing the nursery rhyme again. When the singing section has ended, the carer signs (and says) 'finished' to let her baby know that the song is now finished and will not be sung again.

D. MOVEMENT ACTIVITY

The baby should always have an opportunity to engage in a movement-based activity. This will allow him to experience playing in a variety of different positions and he will learn the thrill of what it feels like to be spun, upside down, high up in the air, and so on. The carer can repeat the chosen activity several times or until her child has indicated that he has had enough. When the activity has ended, the carer signals the end of the movement activity by using the sign for (and saying) 'finished'.

E. SENSORY ACTIVITY

This section offers a variety of sensory experiences that the baby may never have experienced before. It may also help to decrease a baby's anxiety about experiencing something new or unfamiliar, as the carer will be encouraging her baby to try something new in a secure, loving and protected manner. The sensory activity should be hidden in a 'sensory bag'. The carer should help her baby to explore the sensory object as, initially, he may be fearful or he may not know what to do with it. (The carer should always be positive about the item and not say 'yuk' or 'that's horrible.')

F. 'WELL DONE' SONG

This song prepares the baby for the play session coming to an end. It is also an opportunity for the carer to offer praise to her baby (no matter how he behaved throughout the session). The carer cuddles her baby, then indicates that the session is finished by using the sign for (and saying) 'finished.'

Points to remember

- Always make activities fun by trying to turn each activity into a game.

- Schedule activities in such a way that periods of sitting are alternated with periods of movement.

- Incorporate motivational toys into the play so that the child is engaged and wants to participate.

- Always offer praise when the child is doing well, or even at times when he is not doing anything troublesome, for example 'Good sitting!' or 'That's nice playing!'

- Keep the baby calm but interested in the activities.

- Show no adverse reactions to the textures being introduced. The aim is to make the baby feel at ease and demonstrate that it can be fun to play with the textures presented.

- Encourage and support the baby but do not force him to touch any items if he is unhappy to touch. The carer should touch the item instead and calmly show interest. Respect his wishes and try to reintroduce the disfavoured item at a later time.

- Talk to the baby reassuringly and let him know what is about to happen.

- Speak in a soothing, gentle, calm manner.

- Use signs or basic gestures to help the baby focus on what is being said. Ensure that the signs chosen are used consistently.

- Use eye contact and exaggerated facial expressions.

- Give the baby an opportunity to approach activities in his own time. Do not rush him.

- Have fun and enjoy the quality one-to-one time spent together.

8

Running a Group

Whilst you may choose to run the programme individually in a home setting, it can also easily be run in a group setting, for example at a local clinic or community centre.

Health visitors, or other personnel such as early years practitioners, can follow the step-by-step programme in their own establishment. Any number of children and carers can attend a programme; however, we have found it preferable to run this programme with an optimum number of six children (higher numbers than this can make it difficult to run the sessions in an organised fashion and more materials will be needed).

Each programme session lasts for approximately 45 minutes as we feel that this is long enough for the age range of the children attending. The sessions can be extended by providing refreshments at the end of each programme session so that carers can interact with each another in a less formal capacity. Programmes have generally been offered once per week for eight weeks. However, the professional can decide how and when to run the programme. For example, the programme can run every day for a week, twice a week for a month, or once a week for as many weeks as is required. Children who have a functioning developmental age of between 2 months and 2 years benefit most from attending this programme. This is due to the type of activities that are used in the programme sessions. Some children who are older, but who have a developmental delay, may also enjoy attending the programme (for example, a 3-year-old who is functioning at an 18-month-old level). Audio tracks and videos can be found online at: www.jkp.com/catalogue/book/9781849056564.

Who can run a group?

We have devised a programme which can be followed by any health, education or childcare practitioner. For example, adoption agency staff, social workers, early years workers, pre-school teachers, nursery nurses, learning assistants, private nursery staff, family respite carers or anyone who is involved with babies and pre-schoolers, in any capacity. The programme can be run by any interested adults who are willing to follow the guidelines provided in this book and who wish to develop a greater understanding of the importance of improving the bond between carers and their babies.

Adults must be willing to help all children participate to the best of their ability and minimise the effects of the differences in children's abilities. All children are individuals and should be treated as equals.

Carer involvement is essential for the success of this programme. Helping carers to bond with their baby cannot happen if the carer does not attend with her baby and join in the activities. Written permission should be sought from the parent/carer as a declaration that the carer has voluntarily commited to attend the programme with her child (see Appendix for an Invitation template). We also recommend that carers are actively encouraged to become involved in running and leading this particular programme as they become more familiar with the activities.

It is also beneficial, when possible, for students on course placements to observe and help run the group. Knowing more about the theory behind the programme, and actually seeing the programme in action, will help a student to integrate theory with practice.

Groups in the past have also been video recorded so that practitioners can evaluate the quality of carer/child interactions in a more detailed fashion. Consent would have to be sought from carers prior to any video footage being taken.

Where can you run a group?

The simplicity of the programme means that a group can be run in a wide range of settings. We recommend that the programme is carried out indoors to enable the carer and her baby to focus on each other, and the activity, without distraction (for example, a noisy road, birds chirping, wind and rain). However, the programme could be run outdoors in a suitable location.

Whilst the programme may be carried out in a nursery setting, a community centre or a club would also be a feasible option, provided that there is a reasonably sized room to accommodate all the children and adults. It is also important to consider the location of the setting chosen. If the carer does not have a car she may find it too much of a challenge to get a bus to a remote location. The timing of the programme is also important to consider; for example, if the carer has older children in school, you may not want to run the programme to clash with school start/finish times.

Young children often have an afternoon nap, so running a programme around lunchtime, when they are tired or hungry, may also be an unsuitable time of day. As this programme is run as a partnership between carer and practitioner, we would advise, if possible, that carers are asked beforehand what days and times are most suitable for them to attend the programme. The routine, fixtures, structures and format of the programme should remain the same for each session, in order to allow the children to feel secure and to maintain continuity. This helps to decrease anxieties and prepare the child for the next activity.

The group – start to finish

1. Identify the children and carers who may be considered suitable to attend a group.

2. Talk with each carer to determine whether she would be happy to attend the group with her child.

3. If the carer is in agreement, issue the *Wiggle Giggle Hug and Tickle* Invitation to be completed (see Appendix, page 78). If the carer does not consent to the programme, she will not be considered for the group.

4. Identify the personnel who will assist with the running of the group (for example, teacher, nursery nurse, carer).

5. Set the dates, times and venue, which should be agreeable to all involved.

6. Issue a Confirmation Letter (see Appendix, page 79) to each parent/carer.

7. Identify a Lead Person to run the programme.

8. On the last week, complete an Evaluation Form for every child (see Appendix, page 82), in order to identify any improvements in the child's functional abilities. This will help to justify and provide evidence for running the group.

9. Issue a Completion Certificate to each carer.

Preparation

*   A Lead Person should be identified.

*   The adults assisting should have all activities ready prior to the beginning of each session.

*   The room should be set up for the arrival of the attendees to ensure that the session runs smoothly.

*   Carers should receive a paper copy of each session's activities, as they can then refer to this and continue to carry out the activities at home.

Now you can begin!

Below is a step-by-step breakdown of how to run each aspect of the programme:

'WIGGLE GIGGLE' SONG ●

The goals of this section are:

- to signify that the session is about to start in the form of a song

- to help settle carers and children and help everyone focus

- to promote child/carer interaction by facing each other.

1. Wait until everyone has arrived before starting the session.

2. When everyone is seated in a circle, the Lead Person says hello to everyone and reminds them that they are at the *Wiggle Giggle Hug and Tickle* programme.

3. The 'Wiggle Giggle' song is then sung. Each carer is to sit with her child facing her on her knee and is to interact with her child as she sings.

'HELLO' SONG ●

The goals of this section are:

- to provide an opportunity for the focus to be on one child at a time

- to help others in the group to learn the names of everyone attending

- to encourage sharing and letting go of an object when asked.

1. The Lead Person plays the song so that everyone is familiar with how the song is sung.

2. The Lead Person encourages everyone to face into the middle of the group to sing the 'Hello' song.

3. The Lead Person issues the hat to a child and encourages everyone to sing the 'Hello' song.

4. When the song has been sung to one child, the hat is to be passed to another child for the song to be sung to them, and so on until the 'Hello' song has been sung to each child.

NURSERY RHYMES ● ● ● ● ● ● ● ● ● ● ● ● ● ● ● ● ● ●

The goals of this section are:

- to encourage carers to sing to their child

- to help carers to learn nursery rhymes

- to help identify which nursery rhymes their own child likes

- to make singing fun and reduce anxiety/feelings of self-consciousness about singing.

1. The Lead Person sings or plays the nursery rhyme for that week whilst demonstrating any actions that accompany the song. The Lead Person shows the carer how the child should be positioned at this time, for example child facing carer, child sitting on carer's knee. (The Lead Person may find it beneficial to have a doll/teddy to use to demonstrate positions.)

2. Play and sing the nursery rhyme for the programme session and encourage the carer to sing and carry out the accompanying actions whilst interacting with her child.

3. When the song has finished, the carer asks her child if he would like the nursery rhyme again and the carer is encouraged to look out for non-verbal cues that the child is saying 'yes' or 'no'. The nursery rhyme is then sung once more if the child indicated 'yes'.

4. The carer signals that the nursery rhyme is now finished by using the sign for (and saying) 'finished'.

MOVEMENT ACTIVITY ●

The goals of this section are:

- to have an opportunity to engage in a movement-based activity

- to experience playing in a variety of different positions

- to know what it feels like to be spun, upside down, high up in the air, and so on

- to experience the thrill that movement opportunities can create.

1. The Lead Person explains the movement activity chosen for that session and provides necessary accompanying equipment.

2. The Lead Person demonstrates how the movement is carried out using a doll/teddy.

3. Each carer carries out the activity with her child whilst, at the same time, looking for indications that the child is enjoying the activity or not. The Lead Person can also assist the carer to interact with the child in an appropriate manner at this time.

4. The movement activity is repeated several times or until the child has indicated that he has had enough. When the activity has ended, the carer is to signal the end of the movement activity by using the sign for (and saying) 'finished'.

SENSORY ACTIVITY ●

The goals of this section are:

* to offer a variety of sensory experiences that may not always be on offer to a child in his everyday environment

* to help decrease a child's anxiety about experiencing something new or unfamiliar

* to assist carers to encourage their child to accept new experiences in a secure, loving and protected manner

* to assist carers to use the sensory item in a fun and creative manner with their child.

1. The carer sits down with her child on her lap.

2. The Lead Person hands each carer a sensory bag that has the sensory activity for that programme session inside it.

3. The carer opens the sensory bag and explores the item within the bag with her child.

4. The Lead Person encourages the carer to become creative when using the item with her child.

'WELL DONE' SONG ●

The goals of this section are:

* to come together as a cohesive programme for the last time in the session

* to develop recognition of the end of the programme through a familiar song

* to praise and give reward for attending the programme.

1. The Lead Person plays and sings the 'Well Done' song whilst demonstrating the actions that accompany the song.

2. When the song has finished, the carer is encouraged to sing the song to her child.

3. The carer gives her child a cuddle then indicates that the programme is finished by using the sign for (and saying) 'finished'.

4. The carer gives her child a sticker and praises her child. The session has finished.

Endings

At the end of the block of sessions, an evaluation form should be completed to assess the child's performance and to determine whether the child has made any improvements. The evaluation form can be found in the Appendix.

Based on our experience, an eight-week programme is recommended, but it could be run daily, or for a shorter or longer period if necessary. If opting to run the eight-week programme, we strongly recommend that sessions are conducted in consecutive weeks, in order to provide continuity. Children can find it challenging to cope with change, therefore routine is vital.

Photocopy the Session Planner and fill out the blanks for each week of the programme (see Appendix). The times stated on the planner are simply a guide as to how long you should spend on each section of the programme.

Points to remember

- Always make it fun.

- If the child resists any sensory activities, respect his wishes.

- Turn the activity into a game.

- Sing as you are involving the child in the activity as a distraction to the sensory activity.

- Schedule activities in such a way that periods of sitting are alternated with periods of movement.

- Incorporate motivational toys into the play so that the child is engaged and wants to participate.

- Always offer praise when the child is doing well, or even at times when he is not doing anything troublesome, for example 'Good sitting!' or 'That's nice playing!'

The role of the adult

Adults who are involved in the group should work together to plan, deliver and evaluate the activities. They should endeavour to do the following:

- Keep the children calm but interested in the activities. Children may be more susceptible to becoming distressed or excitable when attending a group.

- Monitor the children closely during each programme session and evaluate each child's performance weekly, adapting further sessions accordingly (see Appendix, page 80). Children may display signs of being overwhelmed by the environment.

- Show no adverse reaction to the textures being introduced. The aim is to make the children feel at ease and demonstrate that it can be fun to play with the different textures presented.

- Encourage and support the children but do not force them to touch any items if they are unhappy to do so. The adult should touch the item instead and calmly show interest. Try to reintroduce the disfavoured item at a later time.

- Talk to the children reassuringly and let them know what is about to happen.

- Speak in a soothing, gentle and calm manner.

- Use signs or basic gestures to help the children focus on what is being said. Ensure that the signs are used consistently.

- Use eye contact and exaggerated facial expressions.

- Give the children time to approach activities in their own time. Do not rush them.

- Have fun, enjoy the programme and develop sound relationships!

All pages in the Appendix marked with a ✓ can be photocopied and be used when planning and running sessions.

NURSERY RHYMES

Here are some nursery rhyme suggestions (there are many more that can be used). Remember to do actions that seem appropriate to the song, stick to them, and have fun:

5 little ducks went swimming one day

5 little speckled frogs

Baa, baa, black sheep

Bye baby bunting

Down in the jungle

Eeny, meeny, miny, moe

Head, shoulders, knees and toes

Here we go round the mulberry bush

Hey diddle diddle

Hickory dickory dock

Hot cross buns

Humpty Dumpty

I'm a little tea pot

Incy wincy spider

Jack and Jill

London Bridge is falling down

Mmm mmm went the little green frog one day

Old MacDonald had a farm

One, two, three, four, five; once I caught a fish alive

Oranges and lemons

Pat-a-cake, pat-a-cake, baker's man

Polly put the kettle on

Pop goes the weasel

Ring a ring o' roses

Rock-a-bye baby

Row, row, row your boat

Round and round the garden

Sing a song of sixpence

Sleeping bunnies

There was an old woman who lived in a shoe

This little piggy

This old man

Three blind mice

Twinkle twinkle little star

Two little dickie birds

Wind the bobbin up

Wee Willie Winkie

MOVEMENT ACTIVITIES

Here are some movement activity suggestions. There are many more movement activities that can be used:

- BLANKET RIDE: Child lies down on his back on a blanket. Carer pulls blanket in varying directions to make the ride exciting and unpredictable. Use phrases such as stop, start and again.

- BOX RIDE: Child sits in a cardboard box and carer pulls box around room, changing direction and speed. Use phrases such as stop, start and again.

- HAMMOCK SWING: Child lies on top of a blanket. Two adults lift blanket up off the ground and swing, jiggle and bounce child up and down in blanket. Sing 'Rock a bye baby on the tree top'

- PEEK-A-BOO: Carer hides behind a curtain or sofa. Child finds carer when carer calls their name. Alternatively, carer could hide their own face with their hands and sing 'I close my eyes, now I can't see, if you are here to say hello to me, who is there, is it you? Peek-a-boo, peek-a-boo!'

- MASSAGE: Start at the shoulders and rub hands down arms to hands. Try with hands, feet and back also. Sing 'This is the way we rub our arms, rub our arms, rub our arms. This is the way we rub our arms, early in the morning' (to the tune of 'Here we go round the mulberry bush').

- NAME GAME: Sit in a circle and roll the ball to one another. Say name of child you are rolling the ball to before rolling ball.

- OBSTACLE COURSE: Use chairs, tables, boxes, tunnels (for example, a bed sheet draped over two chairs) for child to practise going over, under and through spaces.

- ROLLING ALONG FLOOR: Child lies on the floor with legs straight and arms by their side. Carer rolls child several times along floor (child rolls from tummy, to back, to tummy, to back, etc.).

- ROLL OVER BALL: Carer supports child to sit or lie on tummy over a large ball. Child can be rocked back and forth, rolled in a circle or can bounce up and down on ball.

- ROLL CHILD UP IN A MAT: Use a soft light mat, for example a yoga mat (or a blanket as an alternative). Try to roll from one end of a room to the other. (Note: the child should be covered up only to his shoulders. Never cover a child's neck or head.)

- SCARF/BALLOON TOSS: Carer throws a lightweight scarf in the air. Child reaches out and catches it as it falls towards him (chiffon or organza material is very light and therefore travels slowly). Alternatively, use a balloon to help develop tracking and catching skills.

- TICKLING: Carer uses her hands or a feather.

- COPY CAT: Carer pulls a funny face/smack lips/put hands in the air/ stick tongue out, and so on. Does child copy you? Can you copy the faces or actions your child makes?

- TUNNEL TIME: Carer stands with legs wide apart. Child crawls/rolls through the carer's legs. Roll a small ball or item of interest through carer's legs first to encourage child to follow.

- UP, UP AND AWAY: Carer lifts baby high up in the air above carer's head. Baby and carer look at each other in this position.

- ROW YOUR BOAT: Carer and baby sit facing each other and hold hands. Sing nursery rhyme 'Row, row, row your boat' as carer helps baby to rock back and forth then side to side.

- CROSSING MIDLINE: Child sits up and picks up a plastic ring sitting on one side of his body and place plastic ring on stacking dowel situated on the other side of his body. Alternatively, child can pick up an item from one side and post it on other side, for example a shape piece into a shape sorter or a ball into a box/bag.

- REACHING UP AND OUT: Baby sits up whilst carer holds items that are motivating to baby just out of reach, for example carer catches a bubble on a bubble wand and holds to the side, or above baby's head, to encourage baby to reach out of his safety zone and work on his balancing skills.

- BABY AEROPLANE: With baby in a tummy-down position, carer places arms under baby's chest and thighs. Carer stands and holds baby at waist height and spins in a circle. Grade speed of spins depending on baby's mood.

- BABY TUMBLE: Carer sits on a chair. Baby sits on carer's knees and faces carer. Sing a song or say 'Ready, steady, go!' before carer holds onto baby's trunk and supports him as he falls between carer's legs or tips backwards from carer's legs.

- HIGH KNEELING: Place toys on a coffee table or sofa. Encourage child to position himself on knees and play with toys in this position.

Games to play in prone position (on child's tummy)

- Carer lies on her back on the floor/sofa/bed. Place baby on carer's chest and interact face to face (sing, talk, make silly faces, etc.).

- Place a pillow, wedge or rolled-up towel on the floor. Lie baby tummy-down over it. Maintain this position to play, for example knock a stack of bricks over, read a book with baby. Try shifting baby's weight to front, back and sides.

- Carer sits on floor with legs straight out in front of her. Lie baby tummy-down over thighs to play with objects on floor, look into mirror, etc.

- Blow up a body/yoga ball. Lie baby tummy-down over the top of it. Carer holds baby securely in place and gently helps baby rock forwards, backwards and sideways whilst on ball. Carer can also help baby lean forwards to retrieve item off ground, for example a favourite soft toy, a stacking cup, a teething ring.

SENSORY ACTIVITIES ●

Here are some sensory activity suggestions. There are many more sensory items that can be used:

- VISUAL: Mirrors, bubbles, clear plastic bottles filled with water and glitter, food bag filled with hair gel and beads, tinsel, flashing lights/balls, torches, mobiles, streamers, pom poms, food colouring to colour water/bubbles, glow sticks.

- NOISY: Bubble wrap, maracas, tambourine, rain maker, bells, crinkly paper, space blanket, rattle, squeaky toys, bottle filled with dry beans/lentils.

- TOUCH: Cornflour in balloons, corrugated cardboard, feathers, gloop (two cups of cornflour to one cup of water), jelly, non-pop bubbles, paint, wet/dry sand, play dough, putty, electrical massager, textured balls, slime (two cups of soap flakes to one cup of water), Velcro, pasta shapes, beans, lentils, sponges, beaded necklace, food-coloured ice cubes, nature objects (for example, pine cones, berries, conkers, twigs, leaves).

- TASTE: Squirty cream, yoghurt, lemon, orange, lime, chocolate powder, sherbet, popping candy.

- SMELL: Coffee beans, mint leaves, vanilla pod/essence, lavender, flowers.

Session Planner

This session planner can be photocopied and completed prior to starting a group or individual session in order to help you plan each session's activities. Writing the chosen nursery rhyme, movement activity and sensory activity for a particular session, and having it to hand when carrying out the session, can be a useful prompt/reminder for the next planned activity. The times stated to spend on each activity are just a guideline.

SESSION: _____

DURATION	ACTIVITY
5 minutes	'Wiggle Giggle' song
5 minutes	'Hello' song
10 minutes	Nursery rhyme:
10 minutes	Movement activity:
10 minutes	Sensory activity:
5 minutes	'Well Done' song:
END OF SESSION	

✓

Wiggle Giggle Hug and Tickle Invitation

Dear: ....   Date: ....

We all strive to understand our babies but often struggle to work out what they are telling us. *Wiggle Giggle Hug and Tickle* is a programme that helps you to interact with your child in a fun, rewarding and delightful way. Understanding what your baby wants and needs helps to strengthen the bond between you and your baby. This programme gives babies an opportunity to experience singing, movement, signing and sensory activities in a structured and playful manner. We want you to understand, respond to, and enjoy your child in order to give him or her the best start in life. Each session lasts approximately 45 minutes.

We hope that you and your baby can join us!

This is what happens in the group…

1. 'Wiggle Giggle' song: We sit and sing the 'Wiggle Giggle' song.

2. 'Hello' song: We sit and sing the 'Hello' song.

3. Nursery rhyme: We sing a nursery rhyme, e.g. 'Humpty Dumpty', 'Row your boat', 'Twinkle twinkle little star'.

4. Movement activity: We move, for example, rock, bounce, roll, sway, spin.

5. Sensory activity: We explore, for example, bubbles, messy textures massage.

6. 'Well Done' song: We sit and sing the 'Well Done' song.

7. The End: We say goodbye.

If you would like to attend *Wiggle Giggle Hug and Tickle* with your baby, please call *(name)* on *(number)*.

Thank you.

✓

Wiggle Giggle Hug and Tickle Confirmation Letter

Dear: ………………………………   Date: ………………………………

Thank you for agreeing to attend *Wiggle Giggle Hug and Tickle* with your baby. We are very pleased that we can offer you a place.

The group will run for (number) sessions at (venue)

The next session will be:

Date:………………………………………………

Time:………………………………………………

Please try to attend each session if possible. If you would like to contact me before the group starts, please do not hesitate to call.

Name:………………………………………………

Tel:………………………………………………

Yours sincerely,

(insert signature)

Individual Session Observation Form

This form can be completed to make a note of carer and child observations during each session. The form can be completed by the professional alone or by the carer and professional together.

Carer: _____ Child:_____ Worker: _____

	Observations of carer	Observations of baby	Additional comments
Session 1 Date: _____			
Session 2 Date: _____			
Session 3 Date: _____			
Session 4 Date: _____			
Session 5 Date: _____			
Session 6 Date: _____			
Session 7 Date: _____			
Session 8 Date: _____			

Completion Certificate

✓

This is to certify that:

(carer)

Attended

Wiggle Giggle Hug and Tickle

at:

(venue)

With baby:

(baby)

Thank you for attending and we hope you both enjoyed it!

✓

Wiggle Giggle Hug and Tickle Evaluation Form

Please give full, honest answers when completing this form. Negative comments are welcome as this helps to improve the group. This is an anonymous evaluation form.

1. Did you enjoy the programme?

    _____

    _____

    _____

2. Did you understand the purpose of the activities?

    _____

    _____

    _____

3. Will you continue to carry out the activities and songs at home?

    _____

    _____

    _____

4. What did you like the most about the programme?

    _____

    _____

    _____

5. What would you change about the programme if you could?

    _____

    _____

    _____

6. Do you have any other comments?

_____

_____

_____

Please return to:

Name:...

Address:...

Thank you.

Fiona Brownlee

Fiona qualified as an occupational therapist in 1969, and since then she has worked in many fields of practice: psychiatry, orthopaedics and stroke rehabilitation. She has worked for over 25 years in paediatrics (ten of them as Head Occupational Therapist at Westerlea School in Edinburgh). In 1992 Fiona worked in the Romanian orphanages and has since returned for follow-up visits.

She has a strong commitment to supporting students, was a visiting lecturer at university and colleges and has spoken at numerous conferences. She has completed Signalong, Hanen and Solihull training amongst many other courses she has undertaken. She has worked closely with all ranges of disciplines involved in childcare and was on a City of Edinburgh Council team promoting care coordination.

Fiona's last job before retiring was Senior Occupational Therapist with the Children and Families Department in Edinburgh, working as a peripatetic paediatric occupational therapist, supporting young children, carers and staff in the city's Early Years Centres.

In 2009 Fiona co-authored with Lindsay Norris (then Munro) *Fuzzy Buzzy Groups for Children with Developmental and Sensory Processing Difficulties: A Step-by-Step Resource.*

Fiona's particular interest and passion is early intervention, as she has seen at first-hand the damage that can occur when a child experiences a poor start in life. She is actively involved in giving talks to early years practitioners on this subject and oversees classes which promote bonding and attachment. Fiona is currently on a panel for Registration and Adoption in Edinburgh.

Lindsay Norris

Since her graduation from Queen Margaret University in 2003, Lindsay has worked as a paediatric occupational therapist. Her first job was with the Children and Families Department in Edinburgh, supporting socially/emotionally vulnerable children to increase their ability to engage in everyday activities. Lindsay left this post to work for the NHS for three years as a community occupational therapist before undertaking a Senior Practitioner Occupational Therapist job in Edinburgh. Lindsay currently works as a Specialist Occupational Therapy Adviser, providing support to a team of Paediatric Occupational Therapists and Community Care Assistants. Lindsay also spent a summer carrying out voluntary work in Romania, working in an orphanage as a paediatric occupational therapist.

Lindsay has attended various training courses over the years, which have improved her expertise in working with children experiencing physical, developmental, emotional and sensory processing difficulties. In addition to her attendance at training courses, Lindsay provides frequent in-service courses for allied health professionals, education staff and carers. She has qualified as a practice placement educator and is the Practice Placement Coordinator in her team.

About the Authors

85